This Belongs to:

_____

"The author receives no money for her books.
All of the royalties from her children's stories are
donated to Kosair Charities."

Donate to:

Kosair Charities

982 Eastern Pkwy

Louisville, KY 40217

(502)637-7696 Email: info@kosair.org

Tap-Dance, Teddy

D. E. Maddox

Illustrated by Cameron T. Wilson

BK

ROYSTON
Publishing

BK Royston Publishing LLC

P. O. Box 4321

Jeffersonville, IN 47131

http://www.bkroystonpublishing.com

bkroystonpublishing@gmail.com

502.802.5385

Cover Design and Illustrations: Cameron T. Wilson

ISBN-13: 978-1-959543-19-0

Printed in the USA

This book is dedicated to GOD. The giver of all gifts, talents, abilities and blessings.

Teddy likes to tap-dance.

He dances with his sister, Sadie.

They wear tap-shoes and top-hats.

They also tap-dance with canes.

They dance up some steps.

They dance down some steps.

They dance all around the stage.

They even tap-dance in their dreams.

Good-night, Teddy and Sadie.

Would you like to Tap Dance with Us?

The End

Thank you for reading and hopefully, enjoyed Tap-Dance, Teddy. I wrote this book to bring a spotlight on tap dancing but also to encourage movement to sound, music or exercise. Take some time throughout the day to play some music and move to the sound to improve health, fitness and peace. One day, try tap dancing, you may love it.

For more information or to connect with D.E. Maddox, email her at: thea_maddox@yahoo.com.

www.ingramcontent.com/pod-product-compliance
Lightning Source LLC
LaVergne TN
LVHW072133070426
835513LV00002B/90